The Latin American and Caribbean Notebook

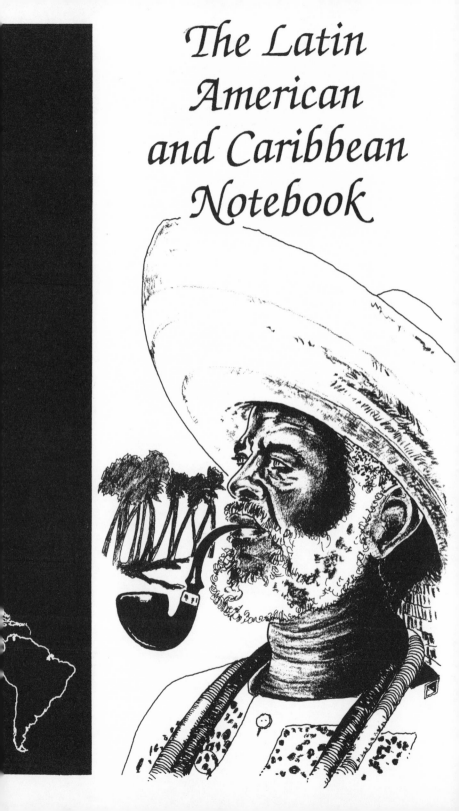

Latin American and Caribbean Notebook, I

Kofi N. Awoonor

Africa World Press, Inc.

P.O. Box 1892
Trenton, New Jersey 08607

Africa World Press, Inc.

P.O. Box 1892
Trenton, New Jersey 08607

Copyright © 1992 Korfi N. Awoonor
First Printing, Africa World Press, Inc. 1992

Cover and book illustration pages by Carles J. Juzang.

Book design and typesetting by Malcolm Litchfield
This book is composed in Adobe Garmond and
ITC Novarese Medium Italic

Library of Congress
Catalog Card Number: 92-70644

ISBN: 0-86543-314-3   Cloth
       0-86543-315-1   Paper

9236-6159

Contents

Dedication

To A.S., with promise and hope

In Memoriam

For friends gone ahead; Joe de Graft, Ellis Komey, Paa Kayper,
Camara Laye, Chris Okigbo, Alex La Guma, Robert Serumaga, and
Geombeyi Adali-Mortty, all the brothers who sang our song,
and went home to the ancestors.

This single line honour roll
weakens, sags, yet longs
for the heady exhilarating hour
of friends and comrades.

Some visit irregularly
like Joe who points out
all the stars in the brightening firmament
to a mumbling recitation
of one recollected evening
Today Israeli soldiers killed a 3 year old boy in
Gaza for throwing stones at military vehicles

And who said that the drama of the dying
wipes out the consequences
and the central theatre of death?

Brothers, your tombs are the verses you carved
on granitic memories;
oh, how I grieve over the tempests
that blew away the young poets
singers of all our songs in this land of fetters.
We promise we shall build the new cities
over your bones,

that your mortuaries shall become the birthplace,
that our land and people
shall rise again
from the ashes of your articulate sacrifices!

Of Home and Sea I Already Sang

Of self too, the intimate details
of creeping age,
the sudden surge of grey,
the uncertain bone, creaky now underneath
a hip, slightly projecting a limp
the Japanese lady in Sao Paolo
said it made the right longer
than the left.

A calm settles
at the beckon of sweet age
and love is sweeter
than the waters of *paraiso*.
Joy and hope soar
for the ultimate task
ahead written about, already
promised in the trajectories of jail,
in absence and exile
envisioned in the immaculate seer's dice.

That we will perform our duty by the people
depose the recalcitrant brutes
and march ahead of our beloved masses
to a coming kingdom.
We have claimed reprieves, honours
vacations, like Sisyphus on leave from his legendary
boulder heaping upon heads long shorn
grains ground by uncertain teeth
threatened by the unsuspecting mint.

I am the circular fire unquenchable,
the drum that plays for the rulers of the earth.
"Kings and Kingdoms shall pass away,
but my benevolence shall not pass away",
once said the preacher.
Grains ground by the pimply professionals,
for pain, let's postpone the meeting time and set
another hour
near dawn preferably,
when calm and dew shall besiege the world
and night tears shall have long dried.

Today the Americans shot down an Iranian civilian
plane over the Gulf of Persia. 290 people including
60 children perished.
President Reagan said it was not his fault.
The fools have closed the western bridge again
So I have to drive around a bend
beyond the lake
past the eucalyptus at sentry
past the waste treatment factory
with the signboard advertising
achievement in stench-control
by the squatter community perched near a ravine
where an accordionist plays
old forgotten sambas without audience
along the superb dual carriage way
to the club to drown my loneliness.

Let the dream not die, master;
Let the dove coo at dawn again,
Let the masthead rear it's head
out of the storm
and share the night with me on this sea.
Let me sing the song you gave me.
Before death comes, master,
Let me dance to the drums you gave me.
Let me sit in the warmth of the fire
of the only native land you gave me.

Brasilia

Of Home Once More

I love a land
in minuscule tear drenched
in misery; but hope
shines on its shores
and denuded hills;
come a time when this love this passion
will not be let die
on thorny fields home or away
but nursed by hope's other sister
fortitude whose strength is the amazing
good for the installation of grace.

Calm now as I steady my boat
for the far but cautious shore;
loves lost, friends dead,
and the refuge in an inane occupation
to keep sanity, receive orders from fools
and pompous jackasses
in the agony of the beloved country
as the dreams we made are rent apart
in ill considered conduct
where once, love, brotherhood
and faith in the wisdom of the people
blossomed.
I steady my nerves for a try
in the soon to come time
when we'll regather the people
for the meal of smoked partridge
around the oblong table of our father.

Soon will come the time
when thru tears
we'll glean the hills
washed clean after the rains
cascaded down our hearts
aches stilled at noon
a time for flames and swords
for arms and strategy,
for victory
        or death.

Rio de Janeiro: Fearful & Lovely City

Indicate a ship
for us to sail to the mimosa fields
through Ipanema, Guanabara
the bay the idiot Portuguese sailors mistook
for the river of January;
small arms industries
bronzed girls in the briefest shrifts
sailing across the crystal sands of a crippled city
blowing *beijos* to the passing world
marooned in hotel rooms on Copacabana
secured by guards
and a whipping wind.
Down in the lower regions, out there,
beyond the glare of the July sun,
the fruit-peddlar hums a tune
to an ailing guitar
of love, pain and absence
of hunger and race despair
in this possible and abundant country.

They come to the fiesta across sand dunes;
the limping habitants of inconsolable *favelas* bring their
music to the *carnavale*
proclaiming that rhetorical *alegria*
they say came from Africa;
infinitude, and plentiful harvest,
co-scavengers roam in bandaged feet,
black and inexorable as my race;
a distant drum beat

the glaze of the light of the primal journey.
on which shores have they landed
on which shores?

The singer was with them
new tuned his descant
rising above the threnody
tremulous like the drums of the afterharvest
across once vast ocean front of home
now shrunk, oh, shrunk
to the sandstrip of childhood memory
marked by the covenant of graves and the cross
brought long ago from Bremen

Oh, sing again my people,
join my song of sorrow, of pain and agony tainted
occasionally with a little joy
that was the signal and the badge
the amulet we wore on this battle ground,
the talisman of our hope and endurance.

Suddenly I feel that surge of age
in a flood of memory of an adage
of survival, struggle, fight and victory;
I feel like doing all the women as I puff my greying chest
pump my muscles into a bulge
and dare the enemies of all my days.

I come again, the braggart loudmouth boastful
uncertain diplomat

after a long season
crafting an answer for the prosecutors
as the Rio de la Plata splashes outside my window,
a lingering southern winter wind
caresses my bones chilled ahead
by the night without sleep in Rio
in a bunkered room they call Luxor

Montevideo—same walk same wall
same old men angling for the shit-eater fish
in the brown murky flow of the Plata.
An idler asked me for time,
mocking once more my negro head
as happened once in B.A. Alex and I.
Each angler clutched his rod.
Two old drunks embrace.
One detaches himself and calls
"Ben Johnson"—the Jamaican boy
who won the 100 km in Seoul and,
wrapped himself in the maple leaf
only to lose the diadem
in an accusing hall of shame. I smiled back
I stop by an antique books store
staring at titles
—rare birds of South America
fly squalling in Spanish, French and Portuguese
not in Guarani or Quechua—
a negro staring at rare books in Montevideo
of rare birds.

The 8th day of spring, yet again
another walk, a last acoustic jaunt
across the listening aqueduct
panoramic sea front—
a palpable negro was pissing against a wall
facing the atlantic of his ancestral home.
Beneath the wall was the legend
"Viva la droga
el sexo e los pena";
the poet forgot to add "la muerte".
There was the incrustable tablet of stone
to Bob Marley *el rei de losoltitos*

I retraced my steps
sad now a little
a setting yellow sun now little
in a half-dip curtesy to the Plata;
the gulls had settled for the night
the negro was drinking his last forgettable
glass of sorrow's wine.
By the locked church I walk, sad a little,
pass Theatro del Solis promising a Brecht tonight
across the *plaza de la independencia*
columns palladian as a Greek's nose,
my last walk perhaps in this city
on this side of this century

Rio—Montevideo. September, 1988

13

Distant Home Country

I appropriate rivers
hills, and lakesides,
seashores used to be my home
in a distant country,
now a narrow strip only
of childhood
memory. I am
rivers and floods
in the ravaging land
of the old continent
and the young country
of tomorrow.

I came to the gate
on an afternoon
before the burial;
mother sat as usual,
in her little casual corner crumbling
near the charcoal stove
ready to cook
all our meals,
sad as always,
mother.

"When I die" she said one noon,
"I wonder whether you will all come
to an empty house".
I played with gods when a boy
took them from Sofe

to the open fields and rivers;
One in particular, elongated head
an enormous member erect,
a god of jokes mischievous as a god
winking at all the perfect pranks of a boy
executed under his charge,
my god, my friend,
to orchard raids, preaching
simple morality to a little boy
in a god and a people's name.

Then I saw Death dancing one noon
with the English lady
with the nasal twang acquired in Adelaide
They danced on the asphalt
outside the winter hotel
on the cold east shore
of the river in that strange city
whose name I cannot recall
at this point of the last sun they danced.
A gull dashed across a bay
where once a sick child drowned dashed,
shrieking.

Agra: January 21, 1989

A pearl,
what I record here
is merely dust
against the red of the fast
and the eastern glare
rising is the mystery of the Taj
in it's majesty.

After Agra,
along the dusty road jammed—
with cattle and men,
memory holding the door now
as I contemplate
the sun and the dust
across a bay recalled again
the Taj Mahal in splendid arrogance
Jihaadists in bows across,
in the imperial mosque
I saw the prophet dusty from the desert
searching for a tree to tether his aging camel.
All the footwears of the islamic nations
placed in rows on spiritual pavements
I record here now, this India,
sad monstrous
        magnificent India.
Remembrance is the gift of the gods
May Allah give us life Allah Akbar Akbar! Ami, Ami.

Cuban Chapters

Santa Clara:
    Written in read and fire
across the soul of this little island
whiffed with pimentoes
and scents of burning cane fields
in barrels of tear and rum.
Jose to Fidel, Che
Camilo Cienfuegos
the many heroes of the vertical hills,
carriers of hope once sealed
in the claws of the northern eagle
once hidden by the fury
of the stripes and banners,
now unfurled in one single starred-bandera
    of freedom!

That evening in December
the wrens came home to roost;
overhead a stormy wind blew
the distance without horizon
laid out beyond recall.

30 years ago, they came here
Che and his brothers;
30 years he stands here tall
after the fall in Bolivia
in the company of iron comrades
who hammered down mountains
smashed boulders and rocks

to re-channel rivers and seas;
around his head now a halo
on his face a vision
in his hand a gun, in his eye a love supreme
    a love supreme.

The Hero's Blood

I know a paradise
when I come into one
of an evening over a hill
on an island
when mountains crouch like lions
and rivers are threads
soaked in the hero's blood
deep dyed in a many tears.

I came carrying a lamp
to see the face of the gardeners
now resting under a *logo* tree

Then a wren came
    fluttering
        seeking respite
from the hunters from the north
the purveyors of righteousness
and death;
I seek a reprieve
from the judges
to bring the herbs missing
in paradise
We cannot die
until we give account
of the freedom day
that shall surely rise
as the sun tomorrow.

Of Faith and Fortitude

On paved seas
and clear blue and liquid marbles
granitic souls of non-believers
shatter the peace of innocence,
in our teeth we hold
firmly unto the bird
in flight, feathers furled
gay bright comrade
of this incontestable choice
to feed my people

And God shall be with his people
This Hopi prayer haunts me still
two decades ago in a far country;
faces of comrades,
many dead now
return to the verge
of personal disasters.
palms, the tall cuban variety,
Marti's symbols of men
Martial replicas of the vertix
of hope
raised on my native ground
seven years ago;
and God is with his people.

The Orient Express

when the poet went to India
January 1989
"He had never fought shy of truth when it was dangerous; nor made
alliance with falsehood when it would be convenient"

Roabindranath Togore on Nehru

That night in Delhi
across a marginal street
strewn with strollers
a loud brass affair came
playing an indeterminate tune.
the groom looking slightly lost
in a horse cart; his relatives nodding to the music
as they led him merrily to the slaughter
far on the northern end of this city of dreams.
The police agitated officious like hens
happy for a procession
tossing their night sticks.
Ernesto Cardenale was having his birthday
64-revolutionary poet priest humanist
combining love of God with love of man.
Agnus Dei qui tollit pecata mundi
Ora pro nobis.

the horses nervous and doped
dance on the midnight air;
soon they vanished beyond a copse;
the hills shade them from us.

21

Betrayers

They planted a dream
My ancestors—in this unselfish gene
self mutilated
      to weep
For those who have not
      share not
For the power men and their brokers
insatiated automatons
of unfeeling worlds
civilized agents of death
horses wizened into second fiddlers
in a vast defeaning symphony
of universal hate.

That I am a nigger is no matter
but that I continue to die
in Memphis, Ullundi, Soweto, Maputo
and Harlem offends my self-esteem—

Their hate, I say, stacked with certainty
even against their mother and birthplace
denying the very feel of the eastern wind
the very torrent of love and pangs
that delivered them
They copyright their sick genuises
in inane poems and self-promotional essays
seek shelter under imperial roofs
citadels of lies and evasions.
more lies compound

their betrayal of our race our land our corn our people.
That was the day the Bombay boy wrote a book
the believers said blasphemed the prophet—
May Allah shine his countenance upon him—
The Ayatollah in his mosque at Qom
pronounced a death sentence.

Then all the hypocritical money-lovers
the historical assassins and conscientious slavers
destroyers of forests and hills
the sackers of cities and homesteads,
plunderers and pederasts
organized a hysteria-
and with the support of the empires dead and new
they beat the drums of war against "terrorism"

I cradled my queen
warm she is my love,
oh memory
she whom I left on the far shores of a river
weeping inconsolably.
the mid age love
to fill a chilling gap
between hemlock and hyssop
between tears and tears
evening dreams wired
in strings of sweat
in an empty alien bed
in an alien far city
I am learning to tie my knots

to pull closer this dispensing wind
to make corporate
this body of my intimate god,
ancestral as memory
tied to many faces now
in anonymous burial grounds
in the now distant birthplace.
I will crush a million mountains
and foothills
flatten cathedrals and temples
to make room for fields
to plant corn for the people

This kingdom where I stash
a memory
green as the remembered home
with the sheep-eye tree in bloom,
the putrescent corpse
in the bush-rat's home
carried aloft by a sad-faced lone murderer
in 43, so long long ago

"an abandoned hospital in South London be-
came a temporary shel-

ter yesterday for a few of the
city's estimated 30,000 home-
less people" writes Peter Murtagh
"Free soup . . . ."

Mrs. Thatcher balanced her books
issued statements on human rights
in Poland, Czechoslovakia and
declared the breaking up of a riotous assembly
of dissidents in Prague
"unacceptable to her Britannic Majesty's Government"
The Black youth of Brixton, Manchester
and the wounded cities of the north wait,
The Irish men of Ulster in jail houses
and in freedom's graveyards wait, wait
for human rights, democracy and free-speech.
"an abandoned hospital in South London be-
came a temporary shel-
ter yesterday for a few of the
city's estimated 30,000 home-
less people . . . ."

Give us this day our daily bread;
in our father's house where
the mansions are filled
with texts of how books were balanced;
impressive statistical data
on the 9th year of economic growth
"an abandoned hospital in South London be-
came a temporary shel-
. . . ."

Havana, Cuba
The Free Territory of the Americas

Arriving in Havana December 1988
I search, I search
the features of the dare
the audace and righteous anger
of Marti's children;
the paling greying stepsons of Antonio Maceo
he who road to battle
with a creaky press;
am searching researching
looking into the faces of the horsemen on the plazas
for the weaning convex metaphor
of death and bravado
in the greying strands of Fidels's beard
he who without saddle or horse
stands taller than Marti's palms
or the remnant pines of Isla de la Juventud,
he who fused the original dream
with the certain vision of youth
dared the eagle in his abominable lair,
wove the red haloes of victory
around the guerrillas' sacred heads
and crested victory or death in rainbows
formed by streams of blood
and the cane-cutter's sweat.
I walked Havana
searching for the men of my village.

I saw them all, saw
the grey old boy with the toothy grin
the mischievous brat with the ample laughter
the buxom girl-bride singing to her child
a long recalled lullaby of the ancestral home;
ah, this brother, with this morning rum
and that, oh, coming sister with erect nipples
and the inscrutable smile of my original hills.

I stretch a hand
across 450 years
of prenuptial night raids
and slave-ships, whips and tears
to you who bore the cudgel scars of my iniquity,
the shame and infamy of my senseless indifference,
you whose tears well and
fall over my eye-lids
as I leaf through the book of degradation;
I swear, I beg of you, I swear
I too stood with you on the auction block
I stumbled with you on the inevitable paths
across marshes and observant forests;
we heard the dogs together
as we hid in the futile caves of trembling;
we heard the clamour of continuing comrades
the din and wail of the brothers
left at home on the African plantations.

From the bowls of cane juice squeezed
from the bones of our mutilated comrades.

we drank a toast to death and exile.
We wept, oh, we wept deliciously,
we wept rivers redolent of the clan and the ocean
that brought us here.

Havana, Havana, how sweet the name,
in the mystic silence of equinoctial nights
recalling struggles—only struggles;
I return to the Isla de la Juventud
renewed by the vigour of foreign youth
all from home—the black remnant continent;
I am still to go to Santiago, Camaguey, Matanzas
to go again to Santa Clara
where el Che stands towering
stern defiance etched by the sculptor's infallible chisel,
Che, who lives in the memorials of a bolivian death
and a Cuban victory.
He speaks, of victories in death not
the dearth of victories.
of struggles, always *siempre* of struggles.

Oh memory, please bring me back to the rivers
I forded, the fields I tramped;
Bring me back, oh, to the village
crush me an orange
bake me a clam
dressed in my favourite peppers
grill me a fat snapper sauced
in the herbs of a thousands forests
served tenderly of an evening

near the palms, a swaying moon witnessing
by my favourite woman, mother
mother, sad-eyed long betrayed by a careless husband
father, self-taught hero
of all my personal tragedies,

Come all of you gone ahead
defiant heroes of a furious fate
at home and abroad
come eat with me this vertical memorial
testament of our collective harvest
swear with me the old oath
that we cannot thirst
when our palm trees prosper
our rivers fish filled
our corbs grained
by he who sends rains and storms
steadies the winds for our determined sails
on a sea mapped for the battle,
he who loves all
sends us farthest afield
to recount the mysteries of his hand

A Caress

So I hang my head
not in shame
but in polite withdrawal
from battles I cannot lose
in the silent impulse
that swats the fly
the gentle touch that weaves
itself a caress
the holding hour of the lover-girl.
of all my days, oh,
she as sweet as the apple-pine
lyrical as an angel
in that village whose name I do not recall
straddling hope
for a better country.

Resurrect all my dreams, my fathers
so I can dream them
for the new people who are coming.

Mortal I am as a little Kingdom
redolent of corporal smells;
but dreams will be reborn
to chase away the ghosts and demons
that frighten the children of our loins
in this land our land
this people, our people.

For Tenu and Afetsi: A Hymn

A crane carried my children
little bright eyed Afetsi, the last tree in the fence,
his brother Tenu, the homestead
is now steady-
inconsolable comrades;
we romped in Brazil once
now only a place of our blood binding imaginings.

Then we heard the generals
and the politicians, leaders
and elders of state
flagmen and ingenous braggarts
scream obscenities on street corners
as winds whirlwinds rose
storms abating
in miraculous hours
of a night remembered
when the children slept
as I cradled them in little balls
till the dying moments
of a fury and a tempest;
of leaders, generals and headmen
once promissory agents of fates
postponed in the hills
along shorelines denuded
houses gone where
the sea eats the land at home
still eats the whole land at home.

Corn as agent
in libatory offerings here, blood, yes
always some blood
part of the covenant with corn and gods
exploring that noon the battlefield
certain that original victories
will be renewed here
in the glowing dusks
and obsolete dawns refurnished
for wars that must be fought
anew and anew again;
blood, yes always some blood,
trickles in menstrual measures
watering births born afore
the kid's mantlers readied
for an outdooring sanguine serious
hurting, but calm,
like the after fury of the sea
that still eats the land at home.
In Havana, now my love city
steeled and tempered in the Fidelista fire,
I raise a voice across time
oceans and chains
against slave days of my life,
ancestral hurts I hurl them back
at all the organizers of my fate.
I reject once more the silence of the manacle
the cooing of the dawn doves
and the bluejays of my Kalamazoo days;
I rejoice in you the girl of freedom

you whom I sang in asphalt cities
and prison yards, you
the refrain I hummed in our forgotten villages

I come again to Havana
23 years to the day
cocky brassy city
where victorious armies hang their banners.

I continue my song, noon song
left unfinished in 66
a half-finished meal
abandoned to sand and wind;
songs are builders' dreams, you said,
architectonic symphonies of joy
or hate or love
irremedial as abortive efforts
at goodness or grace
left in tact in some Sahelian pauper's field
not enough to appease
this millennium old hunger of my people.

Anyidoho in song raised the truth:
we have people,
we too have people.

By what margin of doubt
shall I measure this pain
ineffable historical immense?

herding freedom children into playing fields
under gun nests manned by dogs of war?

I came again into my dream city
Havana, not for the architecture
Spanish American to the core
but to recall my gladiatorial days
in imperial cities
where once I marched
in the ranks of Caesar's armies
I was the dark sword bearer
abandoned in upper Gaul;
centuries later my ancestral shield
was resurrected to adorn
the cathedral at Yamousoukro.

And Frenchmen, though dead
shall tell the fate of Africa-
endorse the name of la Côte d'Ivoire
sublimated by phallic christian temples
against measurements given and demanded
by those whose gunmen
killed us in Lusaka, Memphis, Soweto and Harare.

They come again feasters on negro foetuses
heir bloody banners proclaiming
"structural adjustment, rescheduling of debt"
aid recycled even in the body
of the green monkeys of our homeland
—acquired immunity deficiency—

the syndrome completes the symmetry
of hunger and death

Then they proclaimed human rights
and democracy, yes the rights
of all to die of their chosen ailments,
of hunger in a world richfull
of grain arms beef chemicals and milk.
I wanted to rise and go to Santiago
to see the long nose S.O.B.
who killed Allende
in the name of the American Liberty
and barricaded that freedom city
sung of in moving cantos by Neruda.

what sin is this that endures
slaveships whips chaingangs
and jeering nigger insults forever
in subhuman cities
where we inhabit crumbling tenements
and wear their cast-offs at home
and abroad?
—acquired immunity deficiency syndrome—
the ailment imposed by greed
and death and
green monkeys, innocent
as the dawn that lifted in the Olduvai,
companions in this valley of wills and hope—
of struggle and victory
of victory and struggle

against the equinoctial hate
dark plots and stratagems of power
to win over death and dying.
Keep the faith, my boys
after I am gone.

Of Niggerhood

Memory told me I'd been here before
once upon an age
now lost in ocean water
companioned by flying fish
across a briefer ocean
a much briefer ocean

I this man greying
won little victories
in little inconsequential wars
absorbed immemorial moments
or else forsaken saying
for a leafy plain and open country
beside a little river
running home in my sea.
Give me a place of peace and love along vertical hills
symmetrical with my enduring will,
please give me still to dream and dare;

I lift a fist
in greeting
Love alone conquers all, some fool said,
I wish it were true
I truly wish it were true.

A Death Foretold

Sometimes, the pain and the sorrow return
particularly at night.
I will grieve again and again tomorrow
for the memory of a death foretold.
I grieve again tomorrow
cull a flower across the yard
listen to the birds in the tree.

I grieve again tomorrow
for a pain that grows on
a pain a friend of my solitude
in a bed long emptied by choice;
I grieve again this grievance
immemorial for
    this pain
this load under which I wreathe and grieve

Yesterday I could not go
for my obligatory walk,
instead I used the hour
to recall the lanes, the trees
the birds, the occasional snarling dog
the brown sheep in a penned field
the dwarf mango tree heavy with fruit
the martian palms tall and erect
the sentry-pines swaying
in a distant field.

I believe in the possibility of freedom
in the coming of the bees in summer
in mild winters and furious hurricanes;
I believe in the arrival of American tornadoes
before I go to hunt
on that island of youth
where I smelt the heady smell
of the wild guinea fowl
and heard her chuckle for her child
in the opening light of an April day.

I believe in hope and the future
of hope, in victory before death
collective, inexorable, obligatory;
in the enduring prospect of love
though the bed is empty,
in the child's happinesss
though the meal is meagre.
I believe in light and day
beyond the tomb far from the solitude
of the womb, and the mystical might,
in the coming of fruits
the striped salmon and the crooked crab;
I believe in men and the gods
in the spirit and the substance,
in death and the reawakening
in the promised festival and denial
in our heroes and the nation
in the wisdom of the people
the certainty of victory

the validity of struggle.

Beyond the fields and the shout
of the youth, beyond the pine trees
and the gnarled mangoes
redolent of childhood and prenativity,
I am affronted by a vision
apparitional, scaly
lumbering over a wall
raising a collosal bellow.
His name is struggle.
He is my comrade and my brother
intimate, hurt, urgent
        and enduring.

I will not grieve again tomorrow.
I will not grieve again

The Prophecy from Iran

And the speaker from Iran said to the Philistines of Gaza,
behold, rise and seize the aeroplanes and ships, bomb the
shops of the Christians of the West so that they heed your
plight and prevail upon the Israelites to let your people
go. And the leaders of the Christians of the West in one
great and agonized voice screamed saying ho, ho, ho see how
evil they are, these bad men of Qom and Teheran who in their
iniquity incite vile cruelty against Christians and
peaceful men. Alas and behold the Christians of the West
heard not the cries and the weeping of the children of the
Philistines in Gaza; they heard not the mourning cries of the
dying women and children crushed against the ancient walls of
Jerusalem; oh, they heard not the dying whimper of Allah's
children in the camp of Sabra and Shatillah when the
Christians under the orders of the Israelities, once children
of God, put men to the torch and the fire. They heard not the
 dying cries of the perishing souls of Gaza. And the Lord's
heart was full of sorrow for the children of Isreal
whom he delivered once from captivity
and returned to the land he promised them, for they commit
evil against his children. And His heart was also full of
compassion for the children of the Philistines whose land He
gave to the children of Isreal.
And it was the first day on the new dawn of creation in the
year of our Lord nineteen hundred and eighty-nine in the
beautiful month of May when the grass was green and birdsong
was heard in the land of Tyre and Sidon, in Jerusalem and
Gaza, in Lebanon and Damascus—all under the cross the
crescent moon and the six-pointed star of David.

In Memoriam: Return to Kingston

for Neville Dawes (1926-1984)

Again, we come again to Kingston
to bury Neville, nay cremate
him who fell in Mandeville
victim of neglect carelessness and rum
consign him to the original fire
    that nurtured him.

Memory, Memory,
    you have held the door ajar
these years;
on that day in the cathedral
as we wept on the bier of a brother
ashen, peaceful, silent;
gone like the furious wind of the hurricane month
that gave him to the fire that nourished him.

I met him, an old African
in a village somewhere in Middlesex
sweeping and carting off autumn leaves.
Through all these changing places
I saw my people:

in the slums and cold tenements
on the urine-wet floors of tram-ways
in fields long harvested by their owners
in sad subliminal houses with Jericho's walls
their ancient warrior gait now shuffles

across uneven grounds;
they used to sing once
songs of the native land
of absence
    of family and clan
of heroes who went empty-handed to war;
they sang of nuptial nights
of moons swaying beyond palm trees
of evening fires lit with flimsy twigs
for the gathering warmth of the tale time;
they sang, these men in rags now,
of kings, rulers and true democrats,
of miracle-men who transformed cobras into twine,
of un-believers and God fearers,
embracing hope and the sharing harvest of hope.
I see them now limp across snowfields
fired on storm nights
of blazing friendless territories of exile
and exile tears;
Recall again oh Gods, the fire in my stomach
the same fire we consigned them to
centures ago in Kingston, Alabama, and Port au Prince,

They will come to share with me
the lean bread and the fragile hope of Havana,
the handful of shrimps smoked on slow fires,
the garnished snapper in full green and red.
the lingering faith in a bountiful future.

Neville, brother, I came back.

I met only Maxwell who mentioned your name
and looked sadder than I have ever known him
I came back to your native city
walked in fear of the crouching lions of your blue mountains
shivering of a milignant fever in the barnyard of a slave city
my ancestral woes intact from Africa
etched upon a hill here
my slavery days of collective dance
when we sang in chains of home
across the sea and the equinoctial hour.

I saw them on the edge of spanish town
where Mr. Thomas clutched his ancient pipe
and spat upon the retreating mulatto girl
with the high behind.
King Cudjoe went into the hills
and concluded a disastrous treaty with the enemy.

On Hagley Park I saw my brother
matted hair ruined eyes and yet
a booming voice denouncing the iniquites
of Babylon whilst the distant sea
my mirror and the narrow world my tomb
boom across a bay where the caravels are drowned
that brought me here.

I come again I say
half-clansman of the ritual goat
tethered to a forgotten tree
in a ruined and alien field;

I am the last dancer in the circular team
kicking only dust
after the graceful ones are done,
the jeers and sneers echoing
down the vast saharas of my history
on whose corner
this day, this natal day,
I weep anew
for historical follies I could not shed
abilities I did not realise
victories I did not savour
hopes I did not endure

I salute very warmly, all comrades
far and near,
some who shared dreams with me
and died in foreign lands
some who jumped ship to join the winning sides
in London, Paris and San Francisco
where I once passed
to check my diminishing account
and order the latest models in books

Toasts we drank return
to remind me of serious moments,
of commitments that will not wait
to struggle with the people.
The meals we shared
at early sunset or sunrise
in smoke-filled rooms redolent with conspiracy

and strategies; the whispers we exchanged
the notes we wrote on details of action
and ideological certitudes
revision—of slogans and tactical manouvres;
the flags we designed in silence and secrecy
for malformed and non-existent brigades
marching as to war
determined columns shorn of hope
and cheer; we led a throng
into the same groves of childhood
steered we were on the flat wood
steadied by a single simple choice
renewing we did ancestral oaths
that when our palm trees prosper
we surely cannot die of thirst.

Under the trees, under the trees
and the rain will come and beat me.
I sang that diviner song
long ago at home in levity and jest
again in passion and faith
on podiums and hills,
in the natal village of Asiyo.
I sang that song in the paternal home
sea-front smashed by the sea
demolishing remnants of the German church
original from Bremen in wood
against the christian hymn
"he whom the Lord loves
he sends farthest afield."

We sang these songs before
in the endless seasons of fish
blue-claw and the grinning oyster
the fat horse-makerel and flat-sole
together with the howling salt-water sprat
and the dome-shelled crab loaded
with unforgettable oils-
all, companions of the roasted corn-meal
soaked in the arrogant gusto
of the original fat of the king palm.

We carried our songs into the Easter cities
paschal as our original sin,
into port-towns and open roads,
village lanes, cooper's sheds
and smithy shops where we shod the horse
for the journey at dawn;
we sang before the sauce sizzled
and raged in the morning of the meal day
before the arrival of the christians and the masters.

Then I smelt the rum shops and the cooking
heard a hymn feminine and ardent
"Make a joyful noise unto the Lord"
and the doors of Babylon closed again,
this time behind me
with Neville and I on the freedom train,
going home, yes, going home.

Lover's Song

There was a time under a bridge
in a foreign country, if I recall,
she came shy weapy.
I told her of love
    and of love's sadness
    solitude and an empty bed.

She answered with silence
dropped a necklace into the grass
turned her head to watch a star.
Then she embraced me kindly
and left a pain in the grass.

The Red Bright Book of History

Blood on the Tianamen
verminous flags, an obscenity
of a naked whore bearing a torch
in the harbour of a wicked city;
drowned immeasurable blood
in Beijing

The scrolls are rolled back
We hear anew the trampling long march
Mao and his comrades bright-eyed from Yenan
the red army has indeed crossed the Tatu River
but not every face is smiling!

Gun nests manned by youth
squared against youth in Tianamen
in the place where demons once held sway
the spring wren found no nesting place

Tanks, artillery, the infantry is in town,
the blast of the penultimate hymn
"The East is Red" heard
above the tramp of the funeral march.
Oh China, Tunghuo, what hyena entered the fold
of your lambs
and wrecked the millenium of dream

Tell me into what final purgatory
have they pushed your soul?
You once ate on dunghills, Tunghuo

Your beggars used to line the entrance
of the cavernous tombs of greed
        near the forbidden gates of the sealed city.

But a dawn bright and eloquent
lifted on your brow in 49.
You chased away the querulous nights of pain.
But now Tunghuo, martial tramps
and rattling arms are heard
on Tianamen.

A gate of heavenly peace?
The East is indeed red
now the red army fears indeed the long march!
banners victorious banners
soaked in blood;

The long march is the tramp of death?
the victorious struggle is the death of faith?
and the permanent revolution a blaze of lies?
Tunghuo, Tunghuo, Tunghuo
the talons of the eagle have been paired
the heels of the brave have been broken
Mao weeps inconsolably
among the ruins of Ting.
Tu Fu the original prophet
has moved his little boats
to the Potomac,
        and the Yangtse is mistaken
renamed alas for the Hudson.

Blood, Chinese blood flows
on the Tianamen in the lovely month of June
spring Beijing flowers blooming
on Tianamen square

June 1989

At a Time Like This

That a hut-place is not a shrine
thatched in seasonal days
with dry grass and palm
fronded generously by the maker,
nature's gift to the native earth
all the creatures in their space.

How the skies bleed
on a moon eclipse in 47
when David came home on a market day
in that town where father
kept shop and
made clothes for the village boys.

At a time like this,
I recall the wasted day
the frivolous hour
spent cutting my nails,
the singular melancholy
deaths of family and friends—
the gnawing shame
that I could have done more
for my fellowman and brother.

These hours now recalling the cruelty
the inconsonant ultimate hurt
administered by once-upon friends
grown arrogant with office and power.
We structured a dream, you and I

once along salt-flats at home,
dried river beds strewn
with skeletal remains
of shame and heroic intentions
conch shell-full
of noble gestures marooned
in dry beds our shame.

I will, I swear seek a hill
of infinite tribulations
and particular sins
where rivers of blood tributary flow
and dead men in bone are real
in valleys of crushed dreams
and remnants insects-gnats
smashing each little darkness
my kingdom, outrage,
my morality and little hours of courage
leaving intact my faith and honour,
my blood, my home.
      my name.

When these flimsy tinsels peel off
leaving denuded enamels of bones
stark as age to be disguised
disposable shells of some honourable men
shit-eating s.o.bs and swindlers
purveyors of reversible truths
posing as guardians of the sacred word
and arguable morality,

these creepy flawed timbals
of cacophonous dismay!

I shared tears and sorrow once
in freedom's name, I say,
stood stoutly by friends and comrades,
defended a common turf of faith
    and nation
lost no honour
in the name of no compromise
raised a howl alongside
the victorious army
and wrote my name
in the Red Bright Book of History.

Back with Sandino

The park that harbours the volcano
was shut on the Monday, *lunes* that is;
the gateman enigmatic as his smile explained.
Five years ago the volcano
was deep sulphurous.
On the road from Managua to Masaya
occasional jams relieved
by young soldiers armed with a smile
inspecting car papers
waving us on with a smile unarmed.

Five years the open-eyed smile
condour, a limbless youth
led by a wet-eyed bride
across the road.
The lovers are fewer,
the green is sharper in the new park
against where we placed a flower
twice for Carlos Fonseca;
the wren song of the evening hour
is clearer, deeper
as the last battle steadies
for the final try.
Banner will wave again, comrades
here in Sandino's country
the cry of heroes dying
in volcanic hills,
children and coffee pickers dying
compesinos left only with dreams

of the flat tasteless tortillas
lean ribs caged in struggle
for this piece of the authentic America.

Give them liberty or
oh, give them death.

On the road to Masaya
I saw the sign post to Grenada
where once in your company
I dreamt on a noon
the resurrection of an island
from a cemetary of dead atolls;
the clenching fist
of an island on the blue Atlantic edge
where Maurice died of treachery and greed
before the coming of the North Americans
under a reganite banner
soaked in inconsolable blood.

In Bluefields, a hurricane
came one night
flattened peasant homes and food fields
and hurried across the hills.
Charity, her hands over her head
wept in the ruined city all night
for bread and cover from the equivocal rain
Oh, she wept, and wept and wept;
the christians and democrats,
human rights and amnesty agents

set their collective face
in perfect scorn!
Human rights, human rights!
human rights for those
who will be as we whose
charity is the miracle of the donor's faith
Hurrah! Cesaire said,
hurrah for those, who invented nothing!
I, Awoonor, forded rivers
crossed paths on daunting hills
seeking that Kingdom
promised by my father.
I pawned all my childhood gifts, toys
and certainties for an infinity
of grace and creature comforts
inane hours loaded with fear and loathing
for a fake and living God
hypocritical as a loudly threatening rain
and gaping cannons on the forts
that will either fire or fall.

Managua, June, 1989

Prayer

My hands clasped now as always, my fathers;
I spent counting hours
commemorating this line running
from far away tortuous pillars
in a mudhouse somewhere, somewhere
down that edge of chains and pains
where the birth chamber
in my grandfather's house far away
in Asiyo
Give me patience to last
this penultimate treachery, masters.

I count with you the beads
to the solemn koranic reading
Bissimillahi! Allah Akbar!
permit us grey ones,
to chew through this nut
cracked yet wholed in seeds
ready for the new breeds of my stalwart loins

Teacher, repeat the prayer over my head
repeat that prayer, teacher,
summon again the old man you sent me
remnant my ancestral head
who walks all lanes
flies all skies
fords all rivers with me
buoyed by my original bow
rain-bent by my serpents of Whyddah

in intimate embrace
of that earth that nursed us together.
Ancient one, rest now with me
in alien beds in friendless cities
calm with insomniac nights
with your cool hands and voice;
send me messages of hope and victory
for the time that will surely come.

I saw him last dawn
this ancestral brother and comrade
trailing remants of my umbilical cord
carrying the last bits of my circumcision
scouring the intimate earth
looking again for my oath
and promise,

Again I saw him last night
young as the sun in the morning
blazing shy half musing smile
eyes shut averted, only briefly.

After a little coaxing
he raised up his head
stared into my dreaming soul
awakened once more in me
the tangible embers of the spirit
and the promise.

The Ancient Twine

Certain hours, I, enslaved
by intangible thoughts translated
as love vibes into precise mysteries
and miracles, succumb to an occasional joy.

I came in my time home
avoiding singlular and unique disgraces
embracing skeletal whores and
declaring them stunning beauties.
I smile once at the original folly.

The merciful rain on the verge
of consoling May winds
harbingers of the season of hurricane
and burning fields of cane

I chose a time clear and clean
inimical and lovable
to asssess the ultimate caress
and those steady moments
terminal points in a lifesong
sung at home sweet
and low among alien people

loud together
in a fabric loomed with an ancient twine
threaded here resilient
toughened by mixes of herbs wine and blood.

"Raise the song for me, my Kinsmen
I am gone, I am gone. There is nothing more to be
said."

Seatime, Another

(*for* A. E.)

So I rode
a safer ship
sail-turned tug-rolled
in seas long known of alien coasts
to this apparent safe have.

Who can tell where any bird will fall?

We took you to that island
on the tip of marble hills
with remnant ancient palms and pines
green against our Atlantic.

You were distraught, I saw,
yet expectant of a time of returns
and hope, hesitant yet certain
that the flight of the eagle
shall precede the nesting time.
We will organise our meagre meals
after production days
when we can count every ear of corn.

I recall clearly the cockcalls
of early dawn in that alien city.

What consoling I need to do
I shall do before tears mature

I shall do before tears are let fall.

What consoling I need do
I will do before death,
that intrepid harvester of fields he didn't plant,
comes calling
with his own distinct bouquet of flowers.

What consoling of the people we need do,
let us do it now
as our road will surely end
in the man's inordinate field.

Readings and Musings

I was reading again this morning,
on the loo poet who jumped over a bridge;
I remember the golden legged girl called
oh her name I forget;
but I cannot forget the sunset yesterday
at the Marina Hemingway
I played a demon game
recalled a miraculous place Stony Brook
on that island where I left
all my friends and lovers

Yesterday I quarelled with this girl
not quarrel, well just an argument, mind you
when she thought we will not be good enough
at midnight
and early dawn when I drove her home
to the East of the city
past the abandoned lovers at the sea-wall
locked in perpetual embrace
passed blue-clad policemen
marooned in articulate conical boxes
on the corner of every *calle* or *avenida*
I returned home as the new sun was rising
to seek the certitude of my bed
with my self-esteem intact
and my honour inviolate

Light Hours in Verse

evening settles,
    slow deliberate
over strains from a Ravel symphony,
melancholy, sad, sacharine if you say;
I prop up the second pillow, gently
and recalled a loved one very far away
I read a sign across the ugly wooden frame
full of goblinic images with gnomic tendencies
for a revelation, a premonition
of a road left to be walked.
I have trod gently too many
already, too too many,
taken too many careful steps
Counted too many cautionary winds
read too many threatening letters
walked away from too many fights
and dared too few turbulent storms.

I glean in a supreme prophecy
the tight possibility of a journey
a new course on another road
in another country
where they know my name
so infinitude, light, sad
violinic harmony of a perfect life
(to be followed by a perfect death
long foretold)
sometimes full of love and laughter
intimate hours of enormous joy.

What particular patterns are revealed here
against a crushing blue sky
in worlds threatened by rains
which we feared once
alongside booming cannons
on a prison wall and yard at home
which we no longer fear?

Where a donkey once broke a fence
brayed in the yard awhile
fled across the fields
and was seen no more;

the brief notice said
Sergei Alexandrovich Yesenin
the poet of the revolution
knotted a cord, recorded roses
and took his life in 25
to an ungodly hereafter.
12 years later, General Konstantin Konstantinovich Rokossovky
    was released and reinstated to his military rank,
    —minus his teeth—

Ravelian strains record again
an intimate sorrow and invisible tears.
I will weep no more against the wind
I shall cry no more in the rain.

Time Revisited

Time will wipe us out
inevitably as it does the April bee
or the welling surf of the ceaseless sea;
but there is a renewal point
as precious as the new skin on the cobra
transforming an uncertainty
into the precise shape of the new bud
of the coming corn.

Songbirds I knew as a boy
resing those matutinal hymns
dirge and praise once heard so long
oh, so long ago again
in the red earthed village
in the tree-lined ubiquitous country.

A Thin Echo of Time's Voice

With what can I seal the wound
cover the sores
that gnaw till the marrows
and the heart string
taut and tender unto pain.
Oh, these aches of all absence
memory of the trees at the birth-place
the earth-space ancestral as the name
emptied steadily of those stalwarts
who go, one by one, into the eternal oblivion,
blood-bound heroic singular men
and the women nubile
with tremulous voices
that raised all our dirges at death hour
merciful as God's grace
unto death.

There was the story of the people of the sun
who came one noon harvest time
to steal farm produce;
a farmer surprised them
cut the ropes
and marooned them on earth.

They are still here
Light and red as the earth
the men from the sun.

I remember him well, my last grandfather,
Deku, tall sinewy
spent all his life in the coffee fields
came home with his simple clothes to die;
he went home to his fathers at 90
if anyone can count the years.

There was a thin echo of time's voice
I recall, distinct, fearful
sailing on a wind
caressed by family love and original poetry.
(by family I mean more than husband and wife
        more than three or five)

We shall rise again, I say
we the children of Awoonor and Ashiaghor's houses
heroic defiant glorious
like clenched fists
solemnity was a drug we took
once in sorrow's house
when death made war upon our home
and termites ate the trees in the fence,
that was an age of tears and memorials,
of burials at dawn before the noon sun;
that was the time of recording and recall,
of history and family affairs
redeemed and returned to ancestral homes
only to be scattered once more to despair's winds.

There were some who resurrected the name
the owner of clothes
and installed heirlooms
gave up thundergods found on the high seas
found a dynasty that still reigns across imperial
boundaries.

We know where our arms were stored
where our feet were shod
where our birds and rivers
were kept intact by consoling winds

I, bearer of our heritage
found a crown on a dunghill,
am saddled now with the task
of wearing this sad lonely crown
of hope.

"As Long as There Are Tears and Suffering, So Long Our Work Will Not Be Over," Jawaharlal Nehru

Indeed, looming once again,
tentative, miraculous and certain,
that surging will to march on
against odds and odds
against the prejudicial smirks and sneers
record again the task fulfilled
hoist a banner for the waging battle
march in the ranks of our people,
our black African people, footstools and heroes,
lynched, massacred, chained in alien lands
whipped under almond trees, trifled with, abused,

as long as there are tears and suffering,
our work cannot be over.

The Girl that Died in Havana

I cannot now recall where the cemetary is
being a stranger here. We bore her
on a lofty truck loaded with flowers
she was 19 and weighed very little
Round face, velvet skin, black jet eyes
well, they were closed when I saw her
This little girl my first assignment.

We passed through the door
jammed with soldiers, uniformed, without arms
They had also come for a comrade.
Did he die in a foreign war,
or did he perish in his own bed?
We pased through a long solemn hall
She lay in state, the girl.
Her friends were seated as at home.
One or two wept silently.
There was her friend from Ethiopia
restless and fretful as a mother hen
whose only chick a hawk had snatched.

Someone started a Christian hymn in our tongue
about a Kingdom far away
where there is no suffering
and evening shadows never fall.
They hymn stuttered and collapsed.

We sat stony faced and looked on.
Death the harvester has cut another green fruit yet
in a garden he did not plant.

The time came for us to go
to take her to the burial ground in the strange city;
our convoy, unusually long for this city
where death is no mystery or stranger
and the state orders it neatly
    and efficiently.

We missed the hysteria, the tears
the drinking and the swearing
the serious messages for the gone-befores
here death is a familiar neighbour,
the removal man who clears heroes' fields.

In the cemetary, the handlers
were happy agile around the light body.
She weighed very little
this little girl from Africa
that died in a distant friendly land.

They lowered her gently if a triffle carelessly.
We offered one prayer,
someone poured libation to the ancestors in our tongue.
The grave was a deep concrete cavern.
One or two shed a tear
We left her in the concrete garden
and went away, the little girl
who died in the strange city.

            my first assignment.

Our Pride Alone

I will indeed record
all pains, all joy
I will indeed record
all hurts, all shames.

Then in that penultimate hour
when our pride alone
is not enough
and the edge is close,
and our glorious family name
does not hold even
as it harbours remnants
of slavery, slaver ancestors and wealth
even as it shields hardy peasants
warrior sojourners from old tyrannies.

Some fool recalls a falling star
and the girl he kissed in a bar
in a far country, 28 years ago
of an early summer, returning from Moscow
en route to Paris with Neville, London,
all cities of conquerors, bright
lingering daylights and somnolent nights.

We broke the wings of a duck
alive after the hunt.
Days after it flew away
as my son played with it.

So seals dance in the arctic seas,
dolphins, ancestral as the monkeys
flap about leading us to safe havens
in our tropical oceans.

Resurrect that dream,
the search for the body of the man
I killed, the girl I lost;
suns do dance on the palm leaves
even in the rain; I heard
a tart laugh
on a night, hypnotic as a drug
and I was strengthened.

Dream — Again

for E. B.

She arrived, the dream of a distant home
    and time, shy nubile
precise bird-like gestures
perfect as our morning sun.

Why, someone asked is this thing
so good, generous, oh so good
at this time of age?

memory, I answered; anxiety perhaps,
the need to reconstruct what is missed
over distant hills, seas and time,
eternalise a sunrise and a happy morning
between erection
    and resurrection
of once a time upon a special land
by a unique river quietly flowing home
record the smell of the meal
the aroma of that girl
that tang of that wine
the rustle of that little wind
in that absent tree.
Perhaps it's to recall the memory
of a birth, yours,
on the bare earth of grandfather's house
at Asiyo.

So love this thing blooms again
saying with someone
that when I die
You this thing shall never die.

New Rain

Soon, the sundrenched fields
roar, resonant flowers aglow
made live by the putrescence
of a corpse planted
by a few years ago village skirmish
wherein all victims were forgotten
by retreating enemies.

the clatter of new rain
scatters a few searchers for boundaries
still reeking with the fact of death
on a bright day of week in hell,
or heaven,
as we record a missal
of a childhood once upon a place
when God was white, bearded
        and inexorable.

Do we really like those things
we love, deny those plausible remnants
of pure happiness
        a drinking carousing
        and kissing time
lavish with sorrow
and memory's pains?

How does the worm's kingdown
resemble our particular constructions
of dream houses at sea and river fronts,

besides a lazy water flowing away
     and away?

I embrace each lover anew
of all my days
suspend each hour
of hate, proclaim a reprieve
for a consoling purgatory
a limbo where they say bodies
     are cleansed
hoist the simple fact aloft
that this instance is worthy
needed of record and celebration;
this love is good as the drink
after the rain, incontrovertible nourisher
feeder of our earth for grain
beans meat of the billy goat
for a festival renewal and beginning
for sheer indestructible joy.

Birds on an Autumn Wire

Turning suddenly I saw
the two birds brown green
flit off the wire
swift against a flashing wind
that whipped the silent trees.

I turned away from the rejection
when I looked again
    there stood on the wire
    a solitary bird.
The wind had stopped.

Then I looked again
the wind was still.
I saw five trees
the first half-perched
the last green-black erect
emerging distant from a bank of clouds
defiant as a hill
    on a yielding plain.

The birds came again
    chatty quarrelsome
garrulous against the silent
    watching world.

Then I saw the house for the first time,
a bay window, a grill
an antenae to catch

a sound or a vision?
The keen eye projects a miracle;
the sombre calm world remains
the one eternity
 long teared with sorrow
 long furrowed by the ploughman.

Shamla Hills: Bhopal

It was not that I forgot
or let slip into frivolous substitutes
or daily chores, that I forgot,
nor was it a simple act of neglect
that singular capacity we develop
sure of a place in crowded history
of our ultimate mortality
of age and inevitable deterioration
of arteries, bones, of tissues and blood;
it could not have been that I forgot
the grim harvest of greed on a slope
somewhere, somewhere, Bhophal,
to be precise, Luanda, Maputo,
Njamena, and the many debris cities
Soweto, Mamalondi, Alexandra, all
erected by the masters of historical greed,

On Shamla Hills, I saw a sunset once
with Ernesto, César, and Okara
rosette, brilliant
illuminiating its own eternal certainty
that the work of MAN AND GOD is not done!

It cannot be that I have forgot

Shamla Hills: Sanchi Temples

The Hindustani Latex Ltd. of Trivandrum
placed this advert in the Poetry Festival Journal
Bhopal, January 11-17,

> "For the first time in India
> world's thinnest condoms
> MOODS
> skin-thin luxury condoms
> Nothing else comes close enough."

Gossamer thin angel edge
light like ancestral meals
ritual light,
for how long will they preach
that all India needs
is a gigantic condom?

Somewhere in this vast arena
tragic as sea and air disasters
shipwrecks quakes and deep rivers
cancelled by man-made fate
structured by greed in boardrooms
multi-national as the wood's journey
around a table at which sat God's rivals
ingenious intellects our apocalypse

On Shamla Hills, we breathed air
sulphur clean, sharp paschal avenging

the monks safron-clad shorn
teeth yellowed by betel
original as the deities in the hills
abandoned among chattering monkeys.
that day, on the road to Sanchi
past chemical plants, hovels
bazaars, we edged a road
narrow as the goodness path
sharp, cross, tiringly patrolled
by bored overseers loaded
with discarded overcoats
of some reject mill.

Sanchi, breath-taking valley town
overlooking half-way a stunning plain.
Surely, armies have clashed here,
Mongol, Tartar, foreign warlords expeditionary
forces of some empire
here on the way to a victory
or carnage and death
in a valley green and ripe
with fruit and meat.

From the temples we stood
aghast not at the folly or the grandeur
at man's vision of God,
intricate obscene patterns of his majesty
divinely linked
    on this eternal hill
    of man's desiring.

It was God himself
inevitalbe as the rising sun
who astounds with his striving
on that plain below
his dwelling place once
now at rest in peaceful fields
his meagre and sufficient gifts intact
for his little brown children
on this precious real estate.

Childhood

When a boy, I used to wander off
away from friends and games,
to seek a quiet place in the grass
or under the tree
to ponder in my child's head
the mystery of my being
of the ancestral thunder house of Sofe.

There was a more fearsome house at Gbota
whose dancers came with me to all by dreams,
as I leapt away
    to favourite haunts
squirrel groves protected always
by that uncle who sneeked off
by his own hand.

Where do we go when the world ends?
Where do we go? If we go
do we go with all our people?
To what hills or caves or fields
to what banks or sea-shores?
For each day that dies
    over unfamiliar cities
rebuild my birthplace, my fathers ....

Parting

so sound a note
of a tear dropped at a place
of wailing,
    confirm the prickle point
of thistles, brambles
    the sharp ritual edge
of pain, at parting.

Is that what it means
when we too,
    having soiled our little spot
    loved our lovers
    eaten the last meagre meal
    of seasonal fruits sweet-sour
    in a temporal place
    under our gods, overseen
    by guardian ancestors,
move on to another land?

You will come again perhaps
when I am more ready
when the season is calmer
and the hurricanes avoid our house
and the lights burn more bright.
You will come again my love,
Hasta luego then

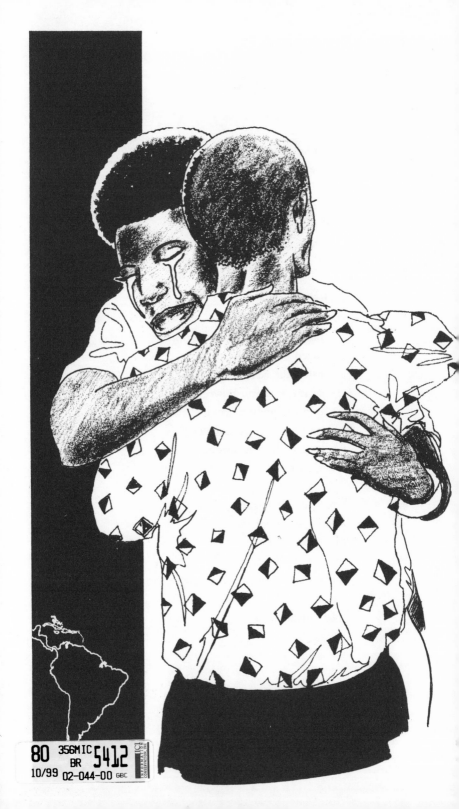